Hello my sweetest dears
There are things I want you to hear
Things I hope you won't forget
And will steer you from regret

I love you Always
You are my "why"
Andrew, Isaiah, Josie, and Peter

To Love I shall testify

Love Is Where You'll Find Me

written by
YVONNE BIENVENU

Love is universal

It is the one unchanging thing

It knows no space or time

It has no boundaries

You, my friend,

are an infinite spark of God's eternal Love

It is Love

    that sent you down to earth

    from Heaven high above

It is Love

    that teaches your soul to evolve,

    to play,

    and to pray

It is Love

    that understands

    we were never meant to stay

Sometimes the people that we love
Seem to drift away
Whether they have wandered just a little
Or have completely gone astray

Always remember that they are
Much closer than you think
So close your eyes and smile
Until your cheeks are rosy pink

Please be sweet and kind
In each and every greeting
And cherish every moment
As it's all so quickly fleeting

You'll grow more in heart and soul
Each and every day
True to self, true to God
Is how you'll live, I pray

Fret not in moments of despair
But know my Love is always there
When you're unsure of where to look
Follow Love's trail to find my hook

Love is where you'll find me
When you're lost or afraid
Keep me in your heart
And I will run to your aid

Love is where you'll find me
To help ease all your pain
Look for me in the flowers and the sun
And even in the rain

Love is where you'll find me
In a cranny or a nook
In a helping hand, toes tucked in sand,
Or inside an excellent book

Love is where you'll find me
When you didn't make the grade
Please know that doesn't hold your worth
For it is Love that never fades

Love is where you'll find me
When you're laughing and at play
I'll be in your giggle and your smile
All throughout the day

Love is where you'll find me
When you're playing on a team
So shake a hand, enjoy the game,
And help build up esteem

Love is where you'll find me
In the big and in the small
Like the warm bright sun above
Or the tiny things that crawl

There is so much awe and wonder
Here on earth's playground
So unplug and be present
To soak up what's all around

After earth's creation
God's real treasure trove was found
Where Love and beauty are beheld,
In us, His golden crown

You manifest His goodness
Down to the last detail
Each with your own mission
To live out what Love unveils

Though my presence will be missed
My devotion to you prevails
Love is in all things pure
For you it will never fail

Love never cloaks itself
In danger or in fear
So stay alert and aware
To avoid the extra tears

When you're feeling sad
(because that's just a part of grief)
Remember my Love is always here
To offer some relief

Love is where you'll find me
In true joy within your heart
Hold still, breathe deep, and remember
I've loved you from the start

Your job is to bring my Love for you
Throughout this very world
To live as an example
For every boy and girl

Our earthly lens is foggy
There's more than meets the eye
If we could grasp Heaven clearly
We'd feel free enough to fly

So holy and so sacred
Is each and every one of you
Knowing Whose you really are
Will steer you from what's untrue

Remember that you my dear
Are a vessel of God's Love
Inspire others to keep their focus
On the things that are above

Let the Holy Spirit guide you
In all the lovely ways
And trust my Love is with you
All throughout your days

So live your life in Love and prayer
And work to do His will
Until you join me once again
In Perfect Love fulfilled

I love you

about the author
YVONNE BIENVENU
OCTOBER 2, 1987 – JANUARY 5, 2022

Yvonne Nicole Goodyear Bienvenu was born and raised in Lafayette, Louisiana. She was an incredibly loving daughter and devoted sister who loved growing up surrounded by many cousins in a large, close-knit family.

She graduated from the University of Louisiana at Lafayette with a Bachelor's Degree in Fine Arts. After college, she married her high school sweetheart, Andrew. During their ten years of marriage, she found her true passion at home as an adoring wife and devoted mother to their three beloved children: Isaiah, Josie, and Peter. Her example of motherhood left a significant impression on many of her friends. Her unwavering and steadfast faith was the ultimate gift she gave her children and this poem is a testament to that.

Inspired by the Holy Spirit, she lived her life as a woman of fierce faith and was convicted that the answer to all things was simple: Jesus. Despite significant pain and suffering, she remained faithful at the end of her life, continuing to find her hope and strength in Christ. As a true witness, she encouraged others to live with an eternal mindset.

Yvonne loved adventure, traveling, and finding beauty in new places. With her creative spirit, she cultivated a home filled with beauty, warmth, abiding faith, and unconditional love. One of her biggest joys in life was warmly welcoming loved ones into the sacred space of her heart and home. With Yvonne, there was no such thing as small love. She was intensely loyal to those whom she counted as family and, if you were a friend, you were also family. Her legacy lives on through her husband, children, family, and friends.

Copyright © 2024 Yvonne Goodyear Bienvenu

ALL RIGHTS RESERVED.

No part of this book may be reproduced or transmitted in any form or by any means, electronic or mechanical, including photocopying, recording, or by any information storage and retrieval system, without written permission from the publisher.

ISBN 979-8-9888588-5-0

This book was prayerfully designed & published by Erin Hawkins Thomas
IN MEMORIAM

created in Adobe Illustrator and InDesign
ERINTHOMASCREATIVE.COM

www.ingramcontent.com/pod-product-compliance
Lightning Source LLC
LaVergne TN
LVHW070433070526
838199LV00014B/498